Family

La familia

lah fah-*meel*-ya

Illustrated by Clare Beaton

Ilustraciones de Clare Beaton

b small publishing

mother
mummy

la madre

lah *mah*-dreh

la mamá

lah mah-*mah*

father
daddy

el padre

el *pah*-dreh

el papá

el pah-*pah*

parents

los padres

lohs *pah*-drehs

sister

la hermana

lah ehr-*mah*-nah

brother

el hermano

el ehr-*mah*-noh

uncle

el tío

el *tee*-oh

aunt

la tía

lah *tee*-ah

cousins

los primos

lohs *pree*-mohs

grandmother
grandma

la abuela

lah ah-*bweh*-lah

la abuelita

lah ah-bweh-*lee*-tah

grandfather
grandpa

el abuelo

el ah-*bweh*-lo

el abuelito

el ah-bweh-*lee*-toh

grandparents

los abuelos

lohs ah-*bweh*-lohs

A simple guide to pronouncing Spanish words

- Read this guide as naturally as possible, as if it were standard British English.
- Put stress on the letters in *italics*.

La familia	lah fah-*meel*-yah	**Family**
la madre	lah *mah*-dreh	**mother**
la mamá	lah mah-*mah*	**mummy**
el padre	el *pah*-dreh	**father**
el papá	el pah-*pah*	**daddy**
los padres	lohs *pah*-drehs	**parents**
la hermana	lah ehr-*mah*-nah	**sister**
el hermano	el ehr-*mah*-noh	**brother**
el tío	el *tee*-oh	**uncle**
la tía	lah *tee*-ah	**aunt**
los primos	lohs *pree*-mohs	**cousins**
la abuela	lah ah-*bewh*-lah	**grandmother**
la abuelita	lah ah-bewh-*lee*-tah	**grandma**
el abuelo	el ah-*bweh*-loh	**grandfather**
el abuelito	el ah-bweh-*lee*-toh	**grandpa**
los abuelos	lohs ah-*bweh*-los	**grandparents**

Published by b small publishing
The Book Shed, 36 Leyborne Park, Kew, Richmond, Surrey, TW9 3HA, UK
www.bsmall.co.uk www.facebook.com/bsmallpublishing twitter.com/bsmallbear
© b small publishing, 1994 and 2012 (new cover)
1 2 3 4 5
All rights reserved.
Printed in China by WKT Company Ltd.
ISBN: 978-1-908164-44-5 (UK paperback)
Cataloguing-in-Publication Data:
A catalogue record for this book is available from the British Library